A Rock and a Restraining Order

Reflections on Psalm 27

Annemarie Poema

WestBow Press books may be ordered through booksellers or by contacting:

WestBow Press
A Division of Thomas Nelson & Zondervan
1663 Liberty Drive
Bloomington, IN 47403
www.westbowpress.com
1 (866) 928-1240

ISBN: 978-1-5127-3397-6 (sc)
ISBN: 978-1-5127-3396-9 (e)

Library of Congress Control Number: 2016904234

Print information available on the last page.

WestBow Press rev. date: 03/25/2016

WESTBOW
PRESS®
A DIVISION OF THOMAS NELSON
& ZONDERVAN

Prologue

I'm a grandmother now, retired from teaching.

It was a Wednesday when pastor asked me to write my thoughts about Psalm 27. I opened my NIV Bible and began to memorize verse by verse.

In the evening I would say my prayers and contemplate the psalm one more time. One morning I woke up and knew I had to draw pictures to help me memorize the verses. So, I began to draw.

Within a week I had drawn all 24 pictures. The Prisma colored pencils went to work next. Coloring, relaxing, loving the light.

May God bless you as you read through this picture book. My prayer is that it brings hope and encouragement to your journey.

Lead me, Lord,

lead me through the intricacies
of this psalm of David.
Let there be healing in the writing down
of words never spoken,
tears never shed.

Bring comfort with the words of the psalm
where your Holy Spirit dwells
and works to strengthen faith
and hope in You
and calm love-worn hearts this new born day.

After ten years of marriage
and two beautiful boys,
the demons of divorce came rummaging
in-between and all around
the edges of our broken lives.
Violence, pain, confusion
permeated the four of us.
The drinking and the violence became unbearable
one cold September, dark cloud day.
As I drove into the sunset, shouting at our dog
to, "go back home,"
I calculated my resources;
two kids,
three diapers,
jackets,
a half tank of gas,
a maxed-out credit card,
thirteen dollars in a checking account,
and monthly income from my job.

Come with us.

"Evergreen" is playing on the piano,
marriage vows are spoken.
Love is sealed with a kiss,
cake is served and the celebration begins.
Watch as love somersaults
through the tumbler
and ends in divorce.

Oh Lord, it is dark.

I come broken,
bruised,
black and blue.

My face bloodied from
another altercation.

Why can't he just give up the keys?

Thirty miles.

Two children.

I'm afraid of the cops,
can't afford another DWI
and I fear another bloody nose
if I speak out.

Oh Lord, turn my darkness
into light.

The LORD is my light

my light

and my SALVATION

whom shall I fear?

depression darkness hospital loneliness despair failure abortion manipulation emptiness kicks bruises paranoia cuts guns

We travel far from the Plains
to the Cascade mountains
trying to run from the shame
and pain of our
"tear-each-other-apart" relationship.

The hours of light are
short in the mountains.
I search for strength
when the sunlight
touches the snow packed peaks.

Can you see me Lord?

Can you hear my scream
at the top of the mountain road
where our camper truck
is caught in a
nighttime blizzard?

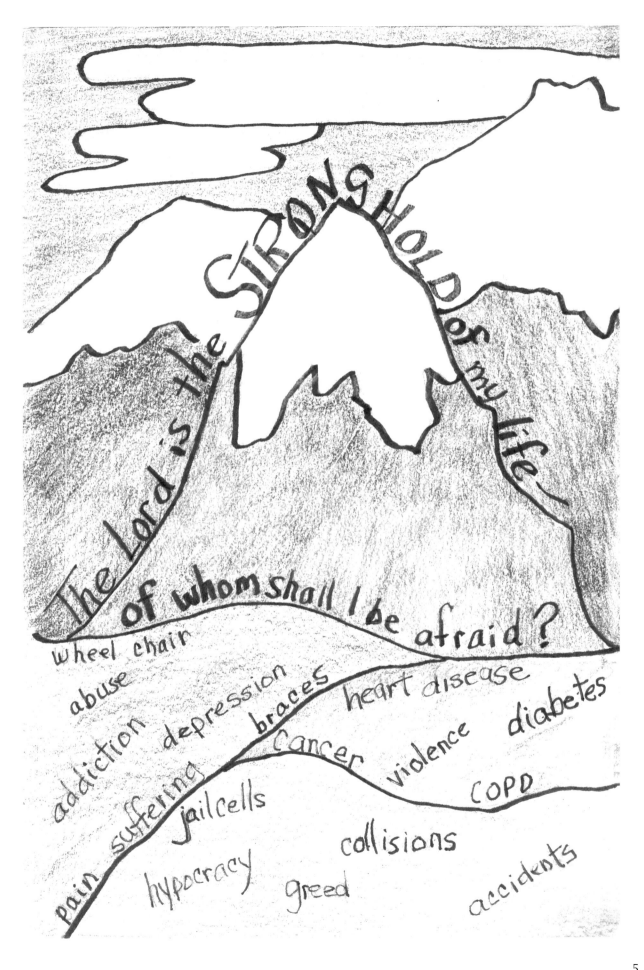

Evil men are everywhere.

The landlord charges too much rent
for the cabin we are in.
Ben wants you to take
just one hit of cocaine.
Rhett wants more than a friendly kiss
at the sight of the double rainbow.
Kent believes he can steal your heart
with a drink or two,
and Barry wants to dance.

Mountain men devour my flesh.

I want to go home.

Just a few beers and
endless coffees,
two packs of smokes,
an argument ensues
and we become enemies.

How does the one you love
become your foe?

I fear I've become an enemy
of my God.

The children are asleep
until the door slams shut.

We all fall down.

There were times in my life
when I was strong.

I declared God's love and protection.

I used to sing praises
at the top of my voice
during college choir and daily chapel.

Now, the army of threats and abuse
has grown.

The longer I am with you
the greater your threats
and the greater my fears.

I am afraid for the children.

On every side
war broke out against me.

A stillbirth on the mountain rock.

A miscarriage.

An abortion that
darkened my world,
broke my spirit,
shattered my heart.

I did not stand confidently
in the heat of battle.

I caved in to his dark threats.

Jesus watched.

Jesus wept.
(John 11:35)

Though war break out against me, even then will I be confident.

"Where's the ocean?"
(Toni Childs)

Where's salvation?
Is there a God?
Which one should I believe?
Will you rescue me?

"Where's the ocean?"
(Childs)

You laugh at me.
Mock me
when I weep tears
of regret and sorrow.

You do not share my remorse
or my shame.

I search and hunger for a Savior.

Tell me there is a cross.

I want to stay here
in the house of the Lord.

Forever.

The world is too much for me.

The one I chose to love and cherish
can not find room in his life
for mercy,
gentleness
or kindness.

He takes my picture
as tears fall
and I crumble once more.

Oh to seek Him in His temple.
To see Christians in action.

Sinners welcome.

Coffee poured.

A handshake, a hug.

A jacket on your cold shoulders.

Bible Study.

Questions welcome.

Friends pointing friends to the
cross of Jesus.

The Lord is in His temple.

Is there a pew for us?

To gaze upon the beauty of the Lord and to seek him in his temple.

THIS IS THE DAY OF TROUBLE.

In a hot electric skillet,
dinner is thrown across the kitchen
breaking the glass in the back door.

Plates and bowls join
the shard-ed mess.

Where are the kids?

Get everyone out!

I pick up the two year old
and run to the patio door.
The seven year old holds up the car keys.
Furniture is tossed my way.
He comes in my direction with a knife.

Grab your purse and run to the car.
We must make it to the
counselor's house.

She has a dwelling for the night.

For in the day of TROUBLE

He will keep me safe in his dwelling;

The woman's shelter.
Our tabernacle for the next ten days.

Volunteers bring groceries and diapers.

We find clothes to wear in
church basement closets.

I file for divorce,
and obtain a restraining order.

The police drive by often.

Money is borrowed,
we are given a police escort
to move our things into a
small apartment.

Our house in the country is gone
along with our hopes and dreams,
our garden,
our tree house,
our barn.

We are safe now,
on a rock.

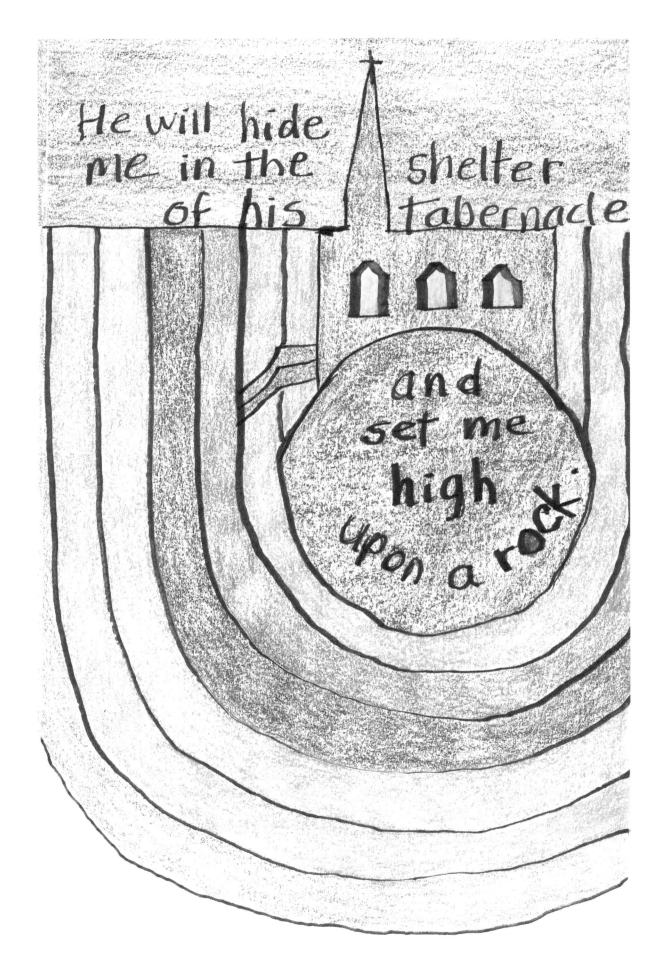

He will hide me in the shelter of his tabernacle and set me high upon a rock.

I must teach the children

NO!

No,
to violence,
hitting,
screaming,
jealousy,
hatred,
anger,
and wrath.

My thinking becomes clear now
that we are safe.

Then my head

anger

adultary

wrath

will be exalted above

murder

the enemies

greed

jealousy who

stealing

Surround me;

idolatry

hatred

envy

coveting

"The dark can give birth to life:
suffering can deliver grace."
(*One Thousand Gifts,* Ann Voskamp, page 99)

We stand ready to be transformed
as only Jesus can.

He transfigures our lives
and takes what is
ugly,
fearful,
painful,
and makes it
beautiful
with a gentle touch.

Thank you Lord for days in the shelter.

"God is always good
and I am always loved."
(*One Thousand Gifts,* page 100)

Glory

Praise

Yes

Alleluia

at his
tabernacle
will I
sacrifice
with
sssshoutsofJoy

Music reveals the turning,
the changing of the soul.

Repentance.

We will sing:

JESUS NAME ABOVE ALL NAMES, (Far From Home)

SLEEP SOUND IN JESUS, (Michael Card, 2002)

I WILL BE YOUR HOME, (Michael Card, 1992)

THE QUIET TIMES, (Kevin Roth, 1992)

NOW THE LIGHT HAS GONE AWAY, (Koine, 2010)

For grace we thank you
with melody.

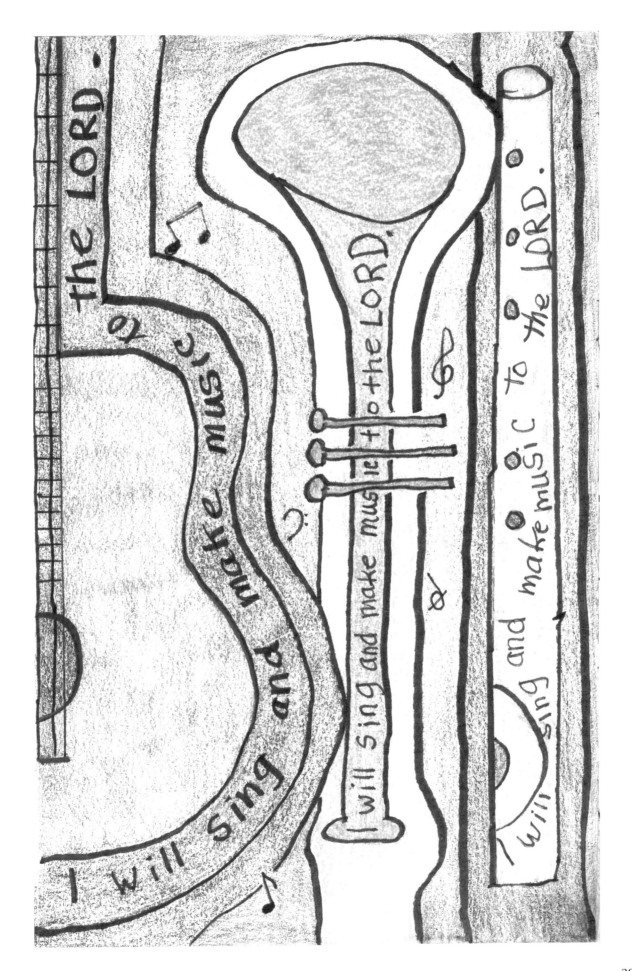

So soon our
multicolored prayers
come trembling.

We have not practiced
being thankful
so we easily become
fearful.

We are alone now.

Empty space at the head of the table.

My right arm missing.

Questions from children
taunt and tease,
"What does your dad do?"

Hear my voice when I call,
O LORD;
be merciful
to me

and answer me.

You brought us up,
out of the miry pit.

We seek your face
and your grace.

We need a gentle smile,
an arm across the shoulders hug
while we seek your face.

The curtain has been torn
and we can draw near.

Become obvious to us.

This crippled family needs you.

Who will change the car's oil and filter?
Mow the lawn?
Water the garden?

Who will show the boys
how to shave
and how to tie a tie?

Open the eyes
of our heart and hands.

Be patient with us.

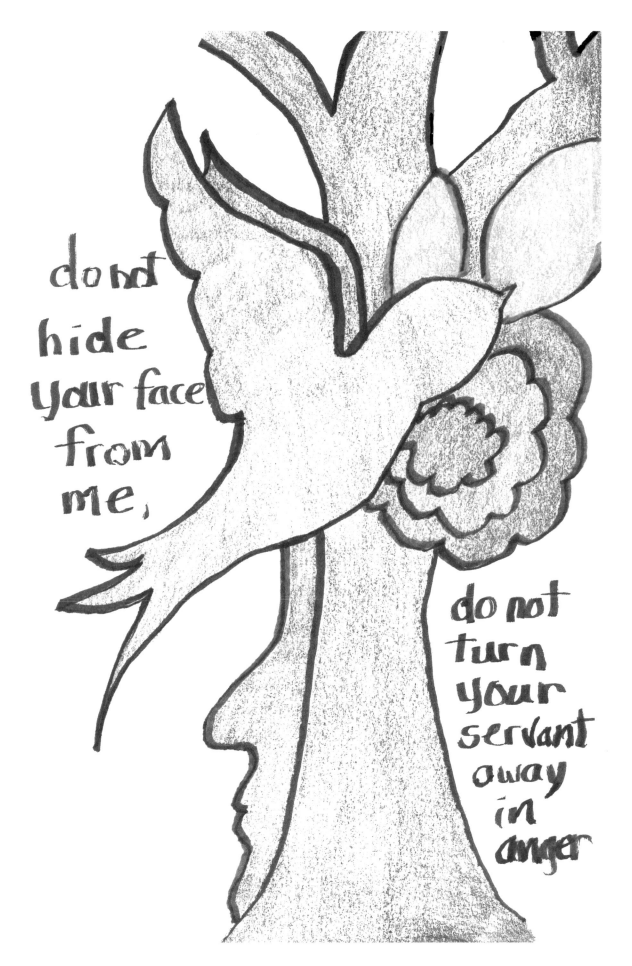

do not hide your face from me,

do not turn your servant away in anger

You led us to the open door.

Let us see the light of love.

We are a thousand miles
from his threats of violence.

We become thankful
for your angels and protection.

Oh God you are my God.

Do not REJECT me or FORSAKE me, O GOD my SAVIOR. You have been my helper.

Where were you
mother and father?

What were you thinking?

We came searching for
shelter,
food,
encouragement,
hugs and thanksgivings.

You gave us a stone.

You left on vacation
and told us to go back
500 miles
and then, file.

There is no room for
the three of us.

Oppressors.

Satan at work
whenever he causes
fear,
doubt,
and shame.

It is hard to focus on Your way
when confusion finds us.

Teach us Lord,
lead me in a
straight path.

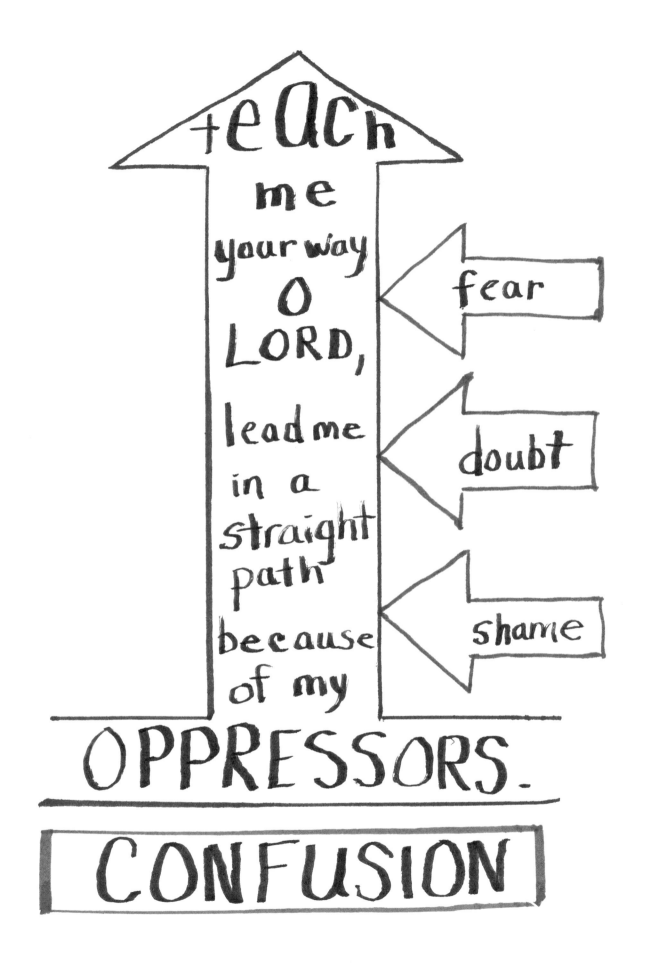

teach me your way O LORD, lead me in a straight path because of my OPPRESSORS.

fear

doubt

shame

CONFUSION

We've learned the way
of a thankful heart.

My foes desire
anxiety, fear,
letting go of thankfulness
and trust in You.

Unlike Lot's wife,
we will not look back
or turn to salt.

One step at a time
we will walk.

Thankful
for quiet,
for calm,
for the turn in the road.

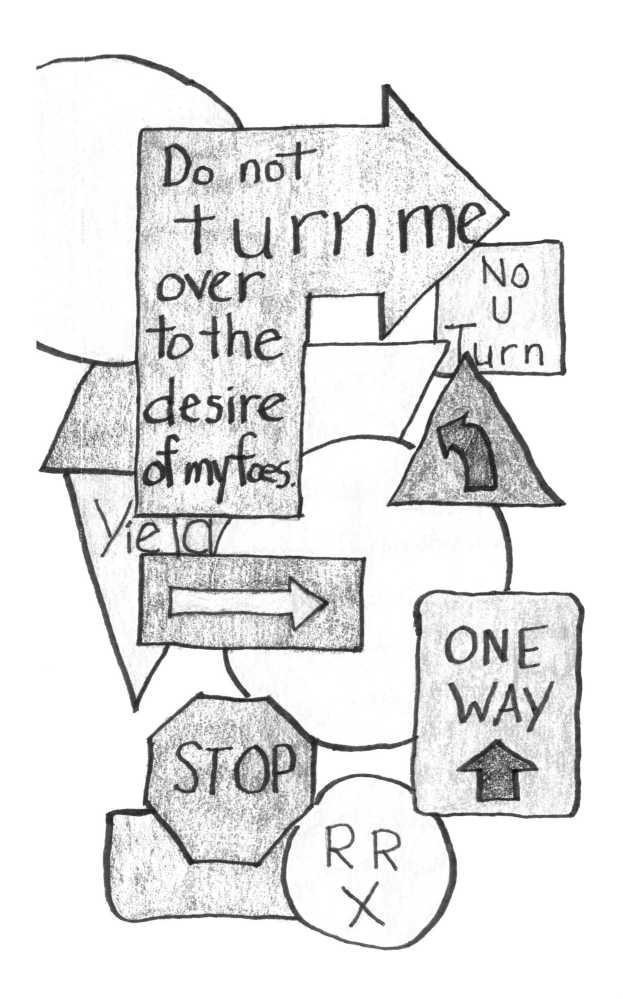

Accusations continue
to be made.

All of the lies
stack up against me
and he breathes out violence.

With every breath a violent exhale.

The children have grown
into thankful men
and we remember to be
thankful for forgiveness.

No condemnation
in Christ Jesus.

for false up
witnesses rise
against me,
Breathing Out
Violence

Now I stand
confidently.

I will yet praise him.

I will wake up.

I will say thank you
for another day.

I eat cheerios and
seedsational toast,
I brew French Roast coffee
and raise thank-yous
for crosswords.

We are thankful
to be in the land of the living.

Thankful for Christ.

I am still CONFIDENT of this:

I will see the goodness of the LORD in the land of the living living living living living living living

Wait
for the Lord;

Be strong
and take heart

and wait
for the LORD.

Wait for the Lord;
Be Strong and take heart

and wait
for the LORD.

Epilogue

It's Wednesday again, near Christmas.
I string the lights on the Christmas tree
and reflect a little longer
as I gently hang each ornament.

How many Wednesdays do we have left?

That I do not know.

I do know the Christ child
is God's love to us.
Messiah.
Savior.
Lord

Printed in the United States
By Bookmasters